The Check Up

Written by Alison Hawes

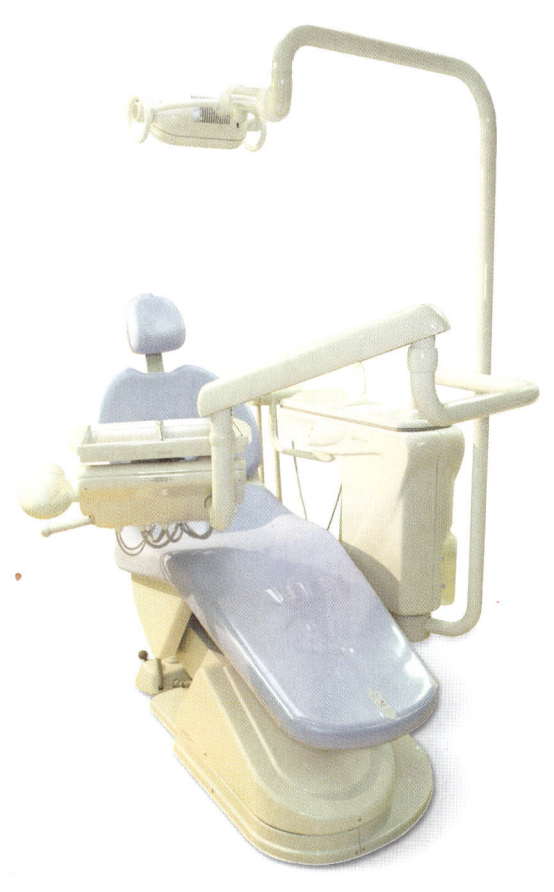

We went to see
the dentist.

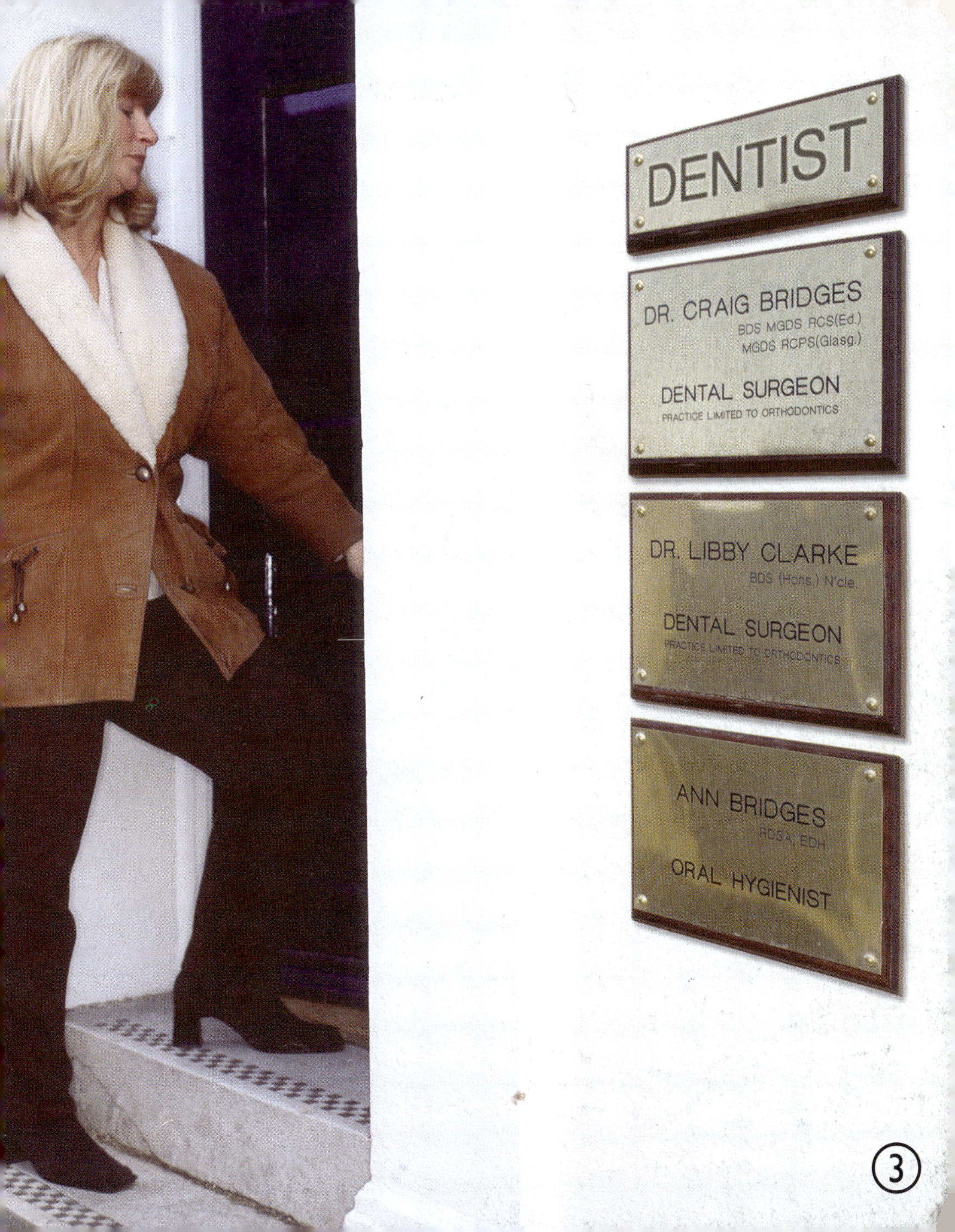

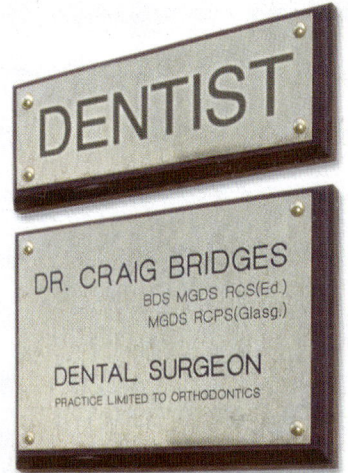

DENTIST

DR. CRAIG BRIDGES
BDS MGDS RCS(Ed.)
MGDS RCPS(Glasg.)

DENTAL SURGEON
PRACTICE LIMITED TO ORTHODONTICS

DR. LIBBY CLARKE
BDS (Hons.) N'cle.

DENTAL SURGEON
PRACTICE LIMITED TO ORTHODONTICS

ANN BRIDGES
RDSA, EDH

ORAL HYGIENIST

We saw the receptionist.

⑤

Then we saw the nurse.

⑦

We went into
the dentist's room.

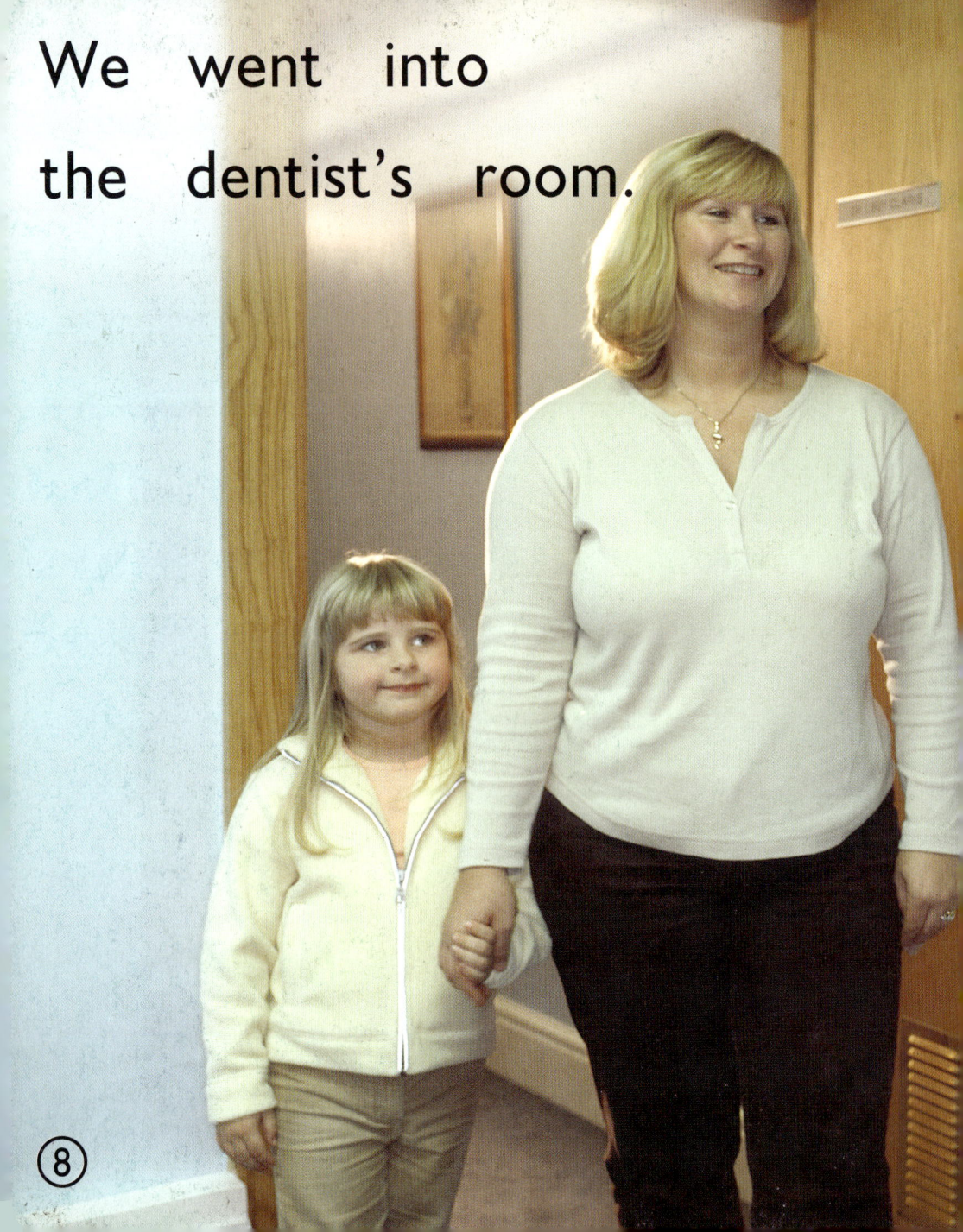

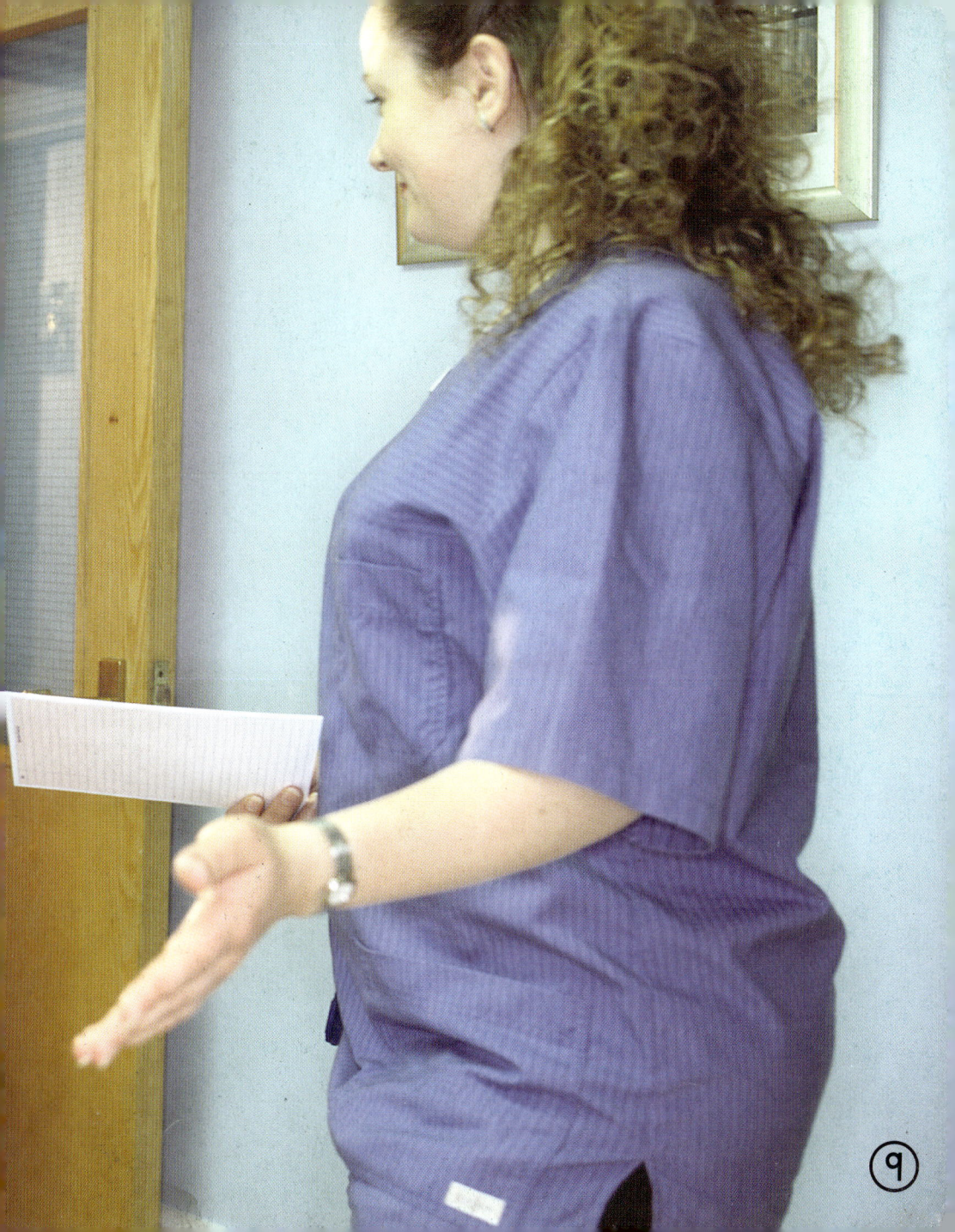

We sat on
the dentist's chair.

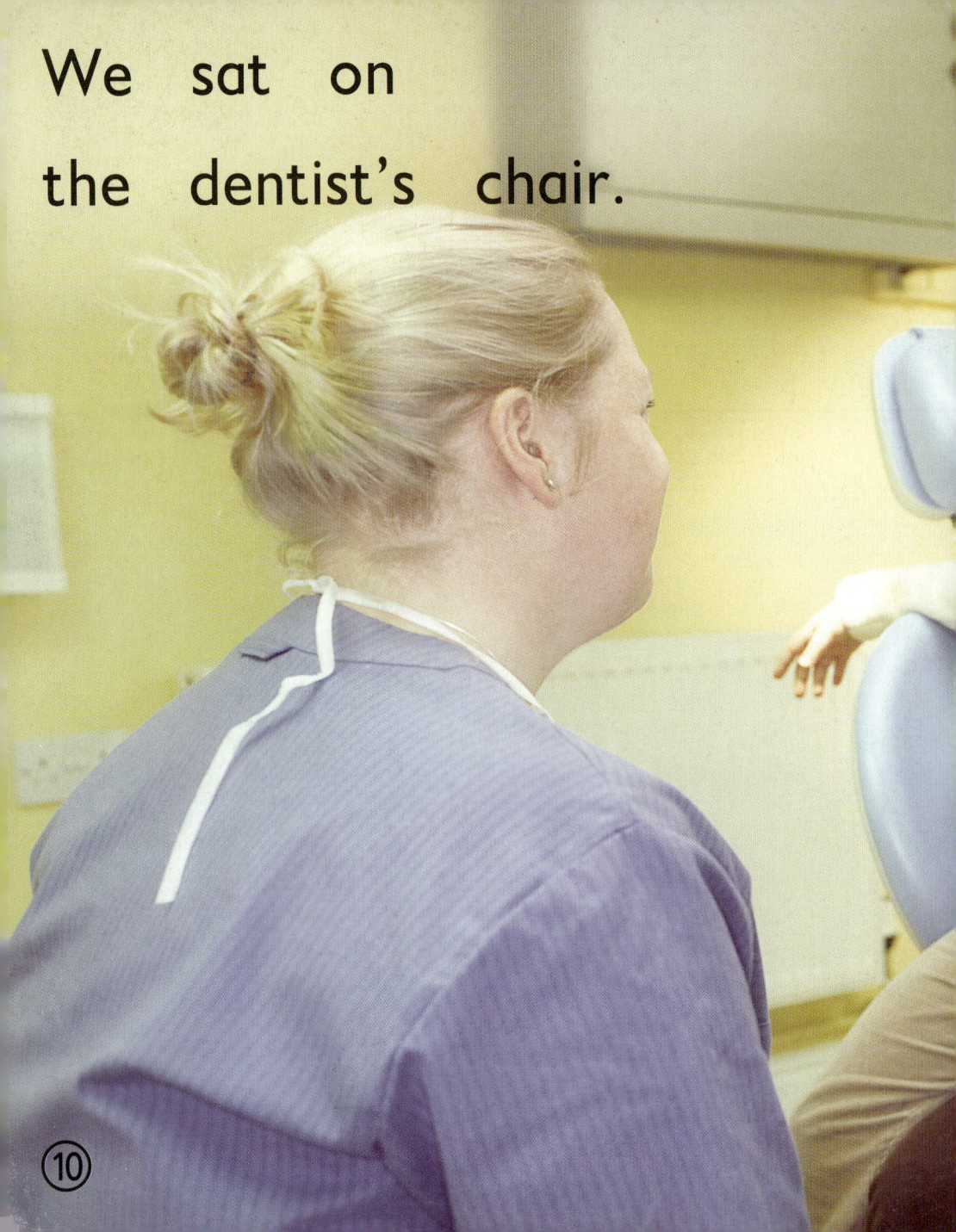

11

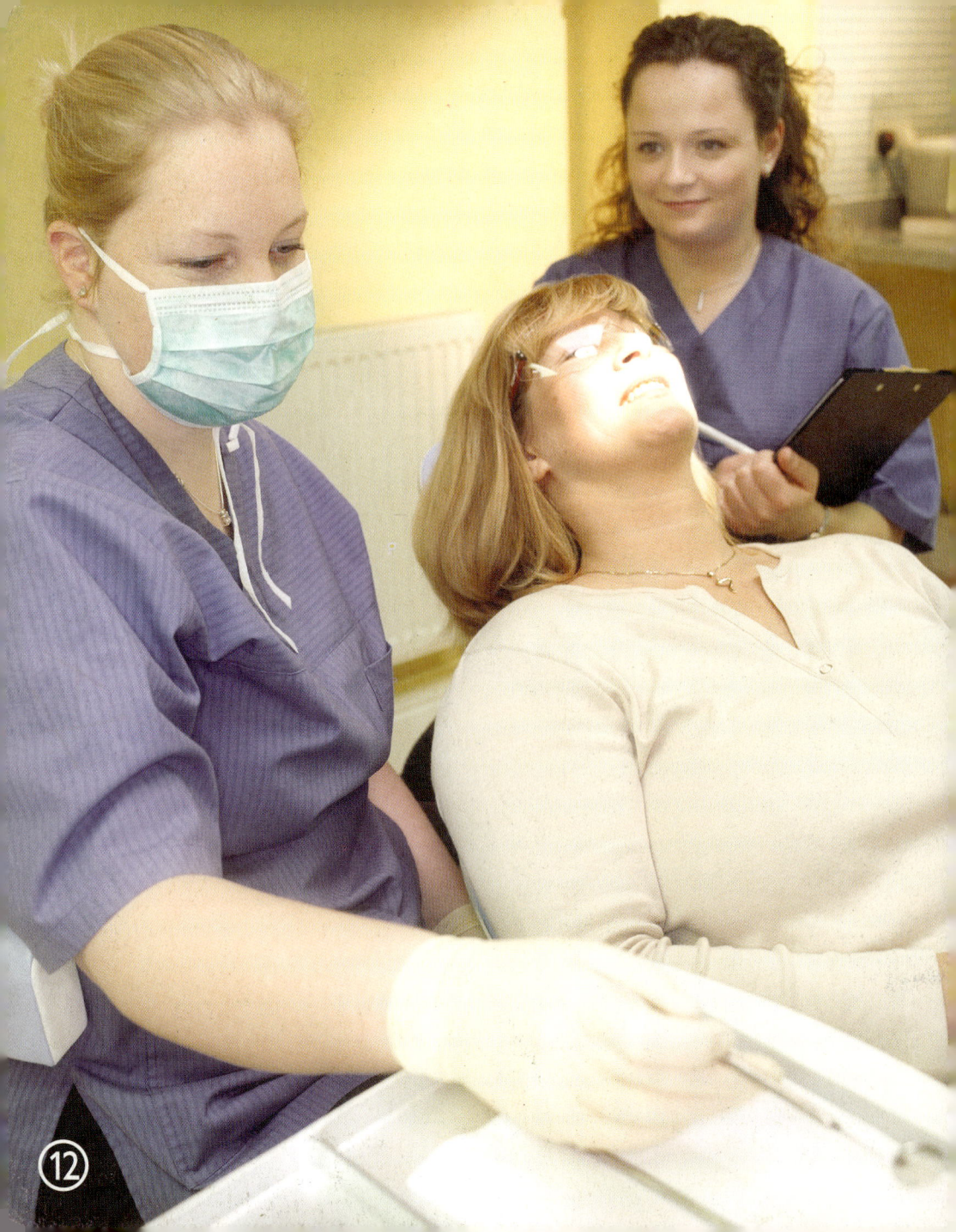

She looked at Mum's teeth.

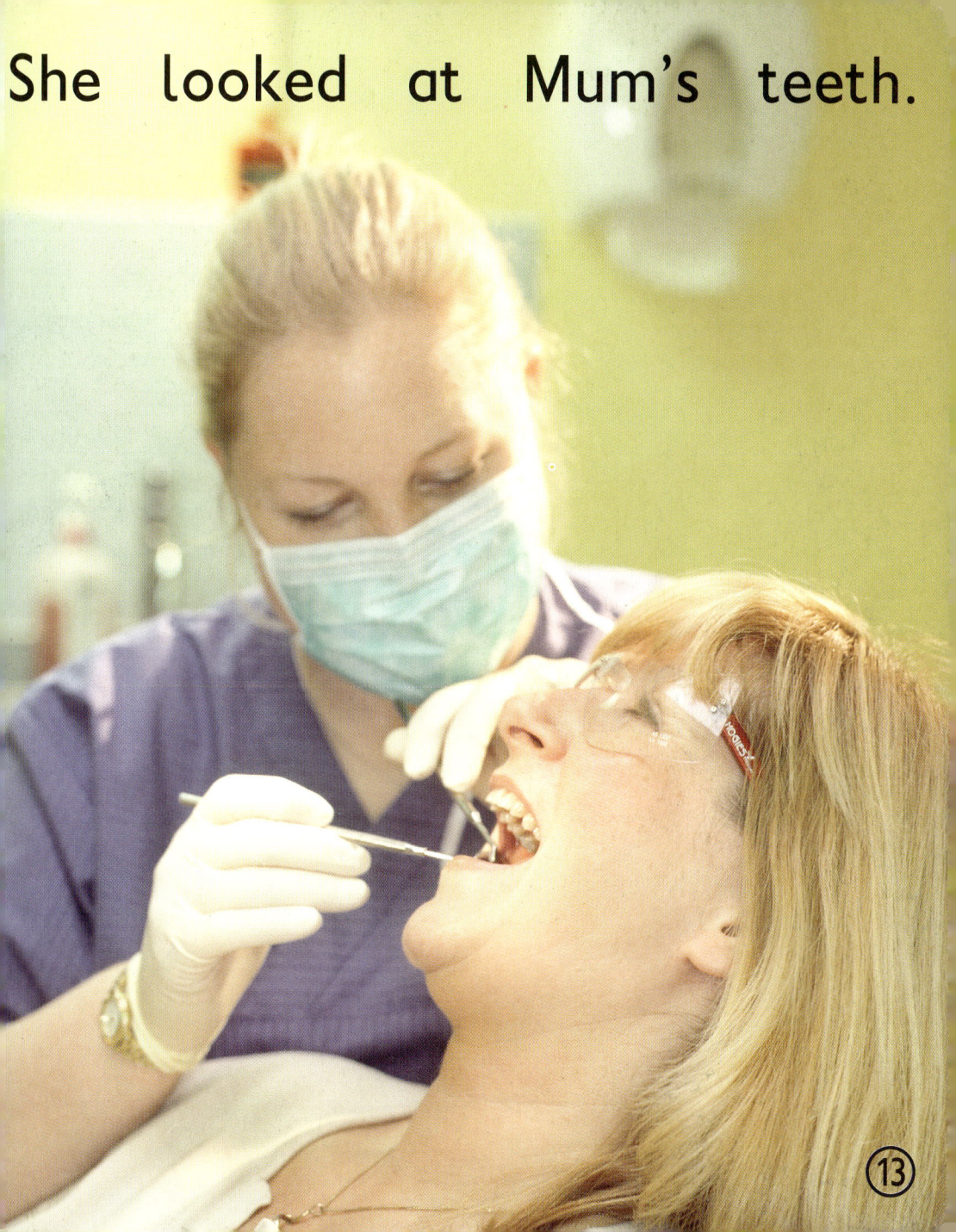

⑬

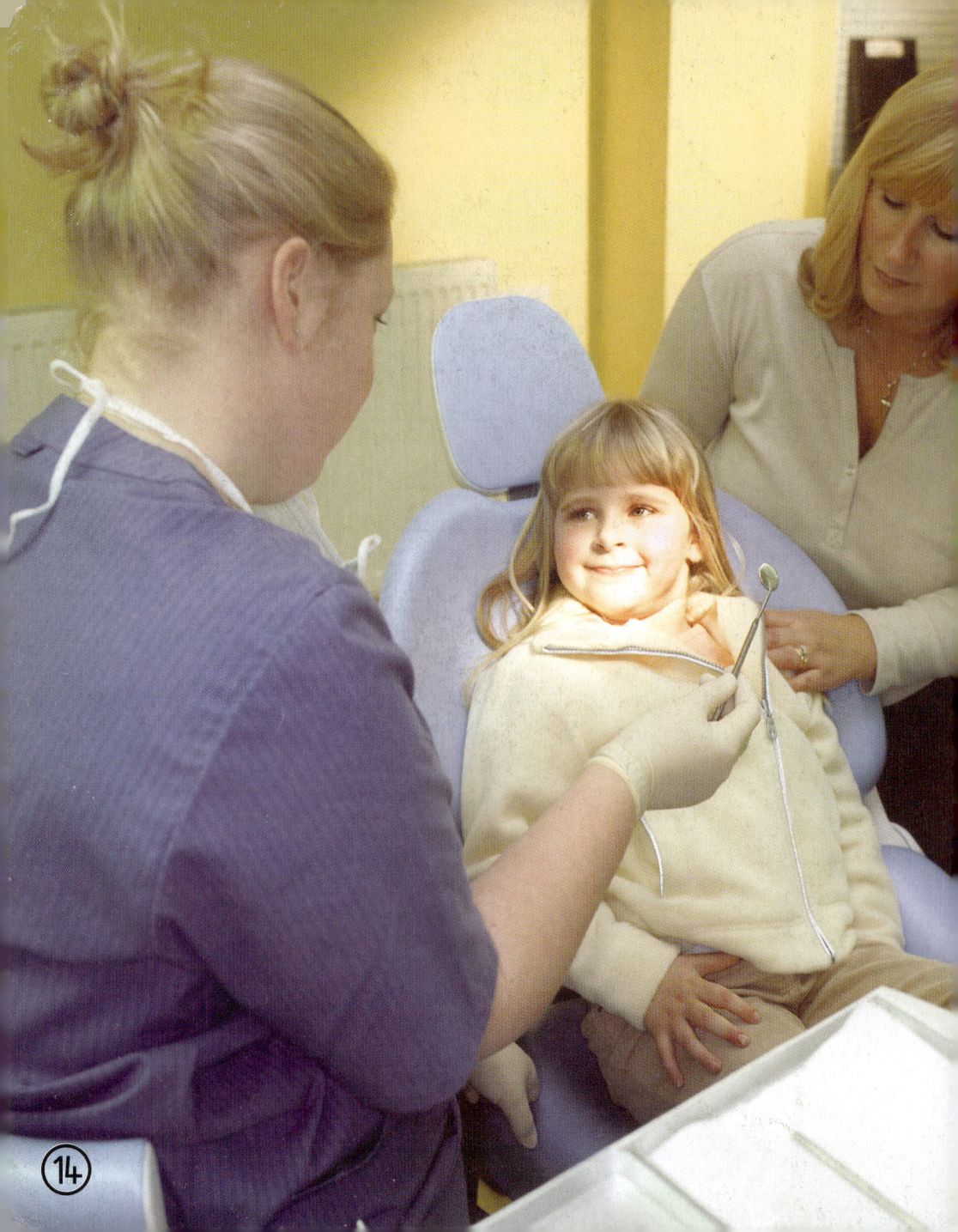

Then she looked
at my teeth.

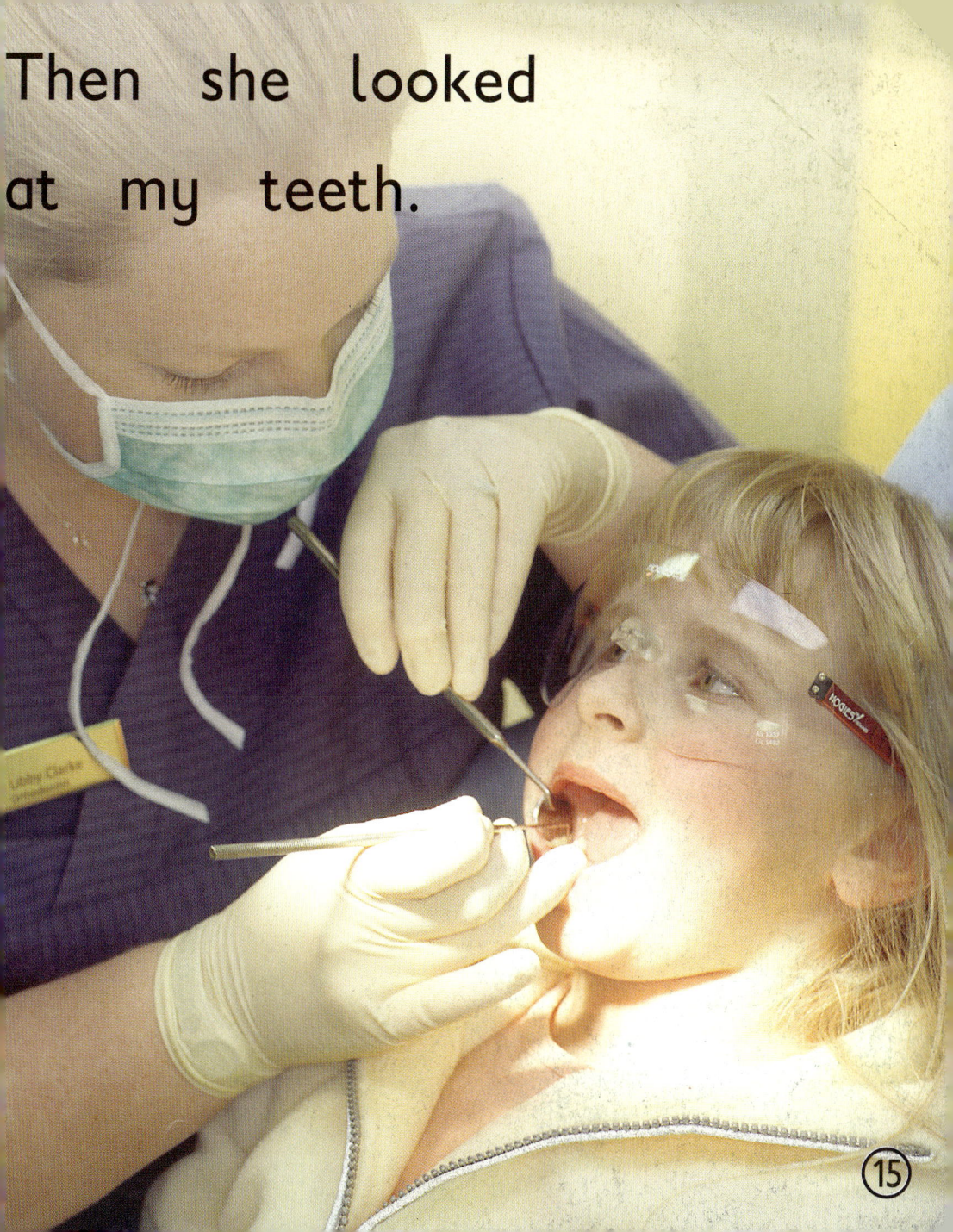

I got a sticker!

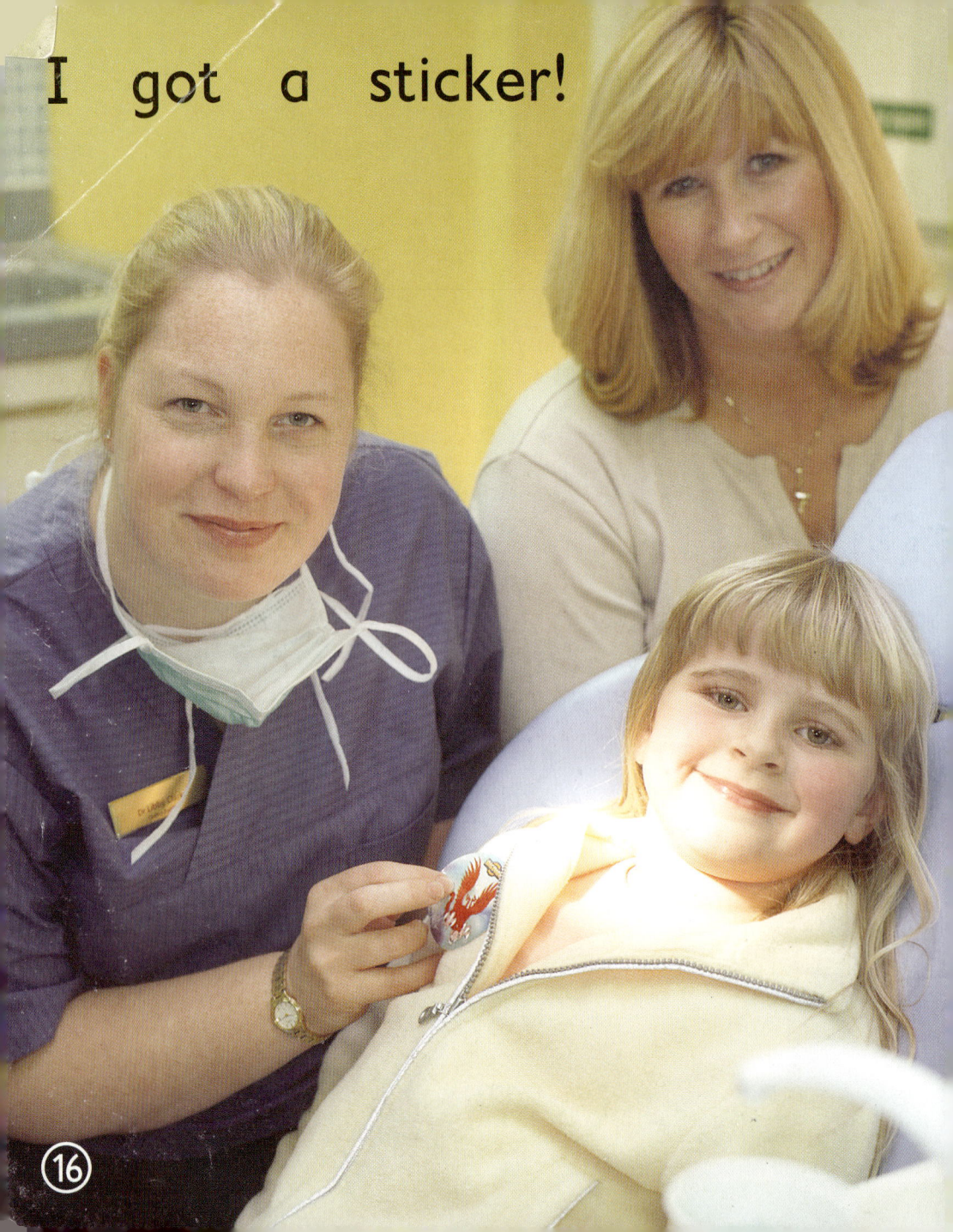